I0759741
NATURAL DISASTER ZONE
VOLCANOES
AND
AVALANCHES
BEN HUBBARD
Cavendish
Square

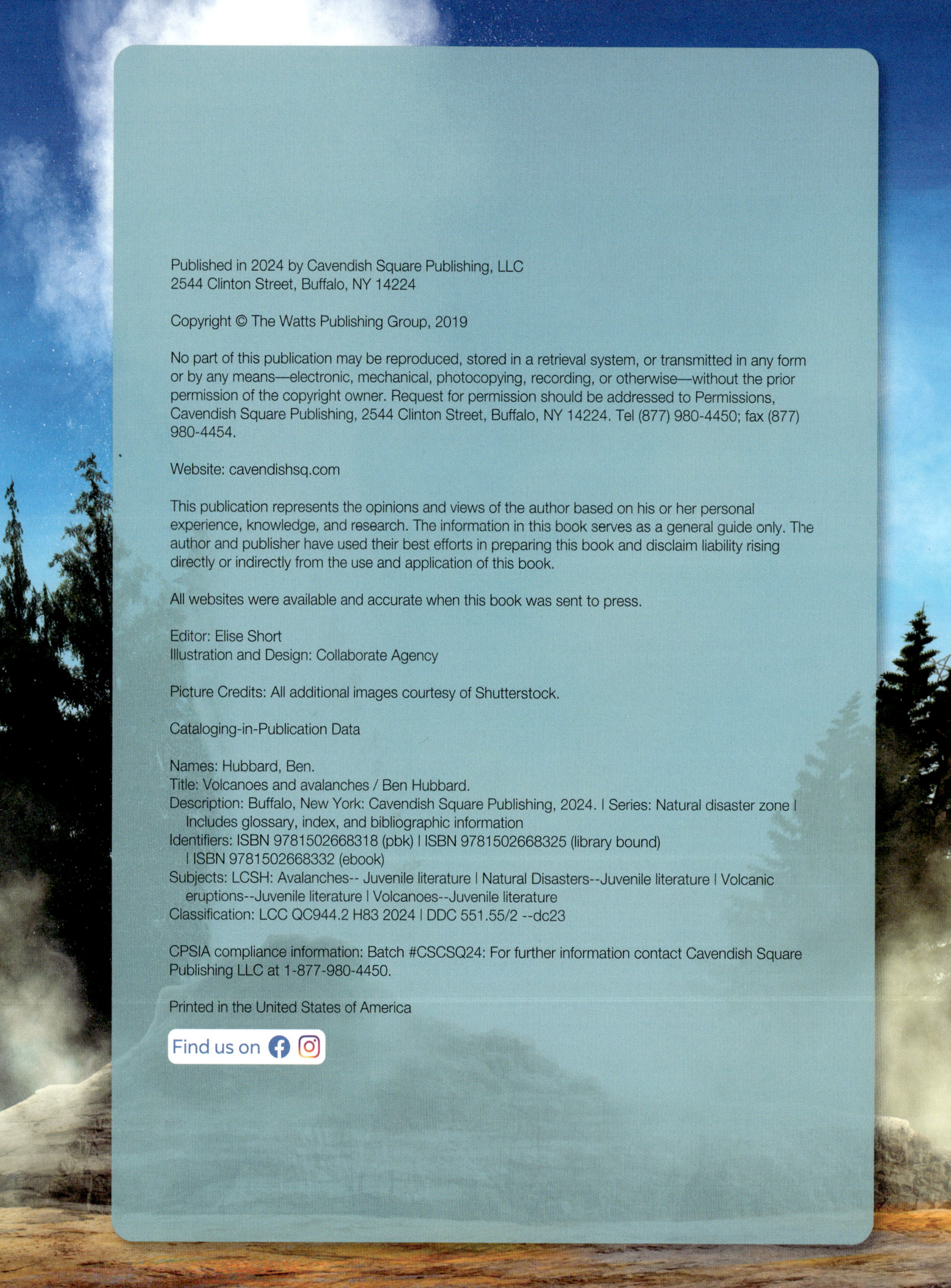

Published in 2024 by Cavendish Square Publishing, LLC
2544 Clinton Street, Buffalo, NY 14224

Website: cavendishsq.com

Editor: Elise Short
Illustration and Design: Collaborate Agency

Picture Credits: All additional images courtesy of Shutterstock.

Cataloging-in-Publication Data

Names: Hubbard, Ben.
Title: Volcanoes and avalanches / Ben Hubbard.
Description: Buffalo, New York: Cavendish Square Publishing, 2024. | Series: Natural disaster zone | Includes glossary, index, and bibliographic information
Identifiers: ISBN 9781502668318 (pbk) | ISBN 9781502668325 (library bound) | ISBN 9781502668332 (ebook)
Subjects: LCSH: Avalanches-- Juvenile literature | Natural Disasters--Juvenile literature | Volcanic eruptions--Juvenile literature | Volcanoes--Juvenile literature
Classification: LCC QC944.2 H83 2024 | DDC 551.55/2 --dc23

CPSIA compliance information: Batch #CSCSQ24: For further information contact Cavendish Square Publishing LLC at 1-877-980-4450.

Printed in the United States of America

CONTENTS

INTRODUCING VOLCANOES AND AVALANCHES

Volcanoes and avalanches are among the most violent and devastating natural disasters on Earth. Both are sudden, extreme, and difficult to predict. When they strike, volcanoes and avalanches inflict very different forms of destruction on the people and buildings around them. So what are these natural disasters?

WHAT ARE VOLCANOES AND AVALANCHES?

Volcanoes are mountains that may explode in fiery fountains of lava, ash, and clouds of searing-hot gas. Avalanches are unstoppable masses of sliding snow, which crash down mountainsides and sweep over everything in their path. Together, volcanoes and avalanches have killed hundreds of thousands of people and caused some of the most terrifying events in history.

Volcano Fast Facts

- Volcanoes are one of the most powerful forces in nature. Their eruptions can be thousands of times stronger than an atomic bomb.
- Ninety percent of the Earth's continents and ocean basins were formed by erupting volcanoes.
- Seventy-five percent of the world's active volcanoes are in the "Ring of Fire," a 2,500-mile (40,000-km) horseshoe-shaped area which stretches around the Pacific Ocean.

Avalanche Fast Facts

- Avalanches kill more than 150 people every year worldwide.
- Around 93 percent of avalanche victims survive if dug out within 15 minutes. After 45 minutes, only 30 percent of victims survive.
- Avalanches often occur during or after a snowstorm that typically dumps over 1 foot (30 cm) of snow on a mountainside.
- Large avalanches can reach speeds of 80 miles per hour (130 kph) within five seconds of being triggered.

When a Volcano Erupts

In September 2010, small earthquakes were reported on Mount Merapi, a volcano on the Island of Java in Indonesia. On October 23, lava began flowing from the volcano. With an eruption imminent, villagers within a 6-mile (10-km) radius were ordered to evacuate. Merapi was about to begin its deadliest eruption in over 100 years.

Fireballs and Gas

On October 25, 2010, Merapi began a series of explosive eruptions that blasted fireballs, ash, and lava 4 miles (6 km) into the air. The volcano also sent a searing 1,472°F (800°C) cloud of gas down its densely populated slopes. As it reached speeds of 60 mph (100 kph), this cloud burned trees, homes, and locals trying to escape. It then blanketed villages 9 miles (15 km) away in 8 inches (20 cm) of ash.

The Human Impact

By November 11, over 350,000 evacuated people were living in cramped emergency shelters in an exclusion zone 12 miles (20 km) from Merapi's summit.

Many villagers died when they returned to check on livestock and were caught up in new eruptions. By the time the eruptions eased on November 17, 353 people had died, over 400,000 people were displaced, and 2,200 families had lost their homes.

Faster Disaster Facts

- Indonesia is an archipelago of islands that sits on the Pacific Ocean's Ring of Fire.
- Mount Merapi is one of Indonesia's 129 active volcanoes.
- For days after the eruptions, a sulphur-dioxide cloud rose 9 miles (15,000 m) into the air and grounded planes 1,550 miles (2,500 km) away in western Australia.

WHAT'S IN A VOLCANO?

A volcano is formed when red-hot, molten rock called magma bursts through a weak spot in the Earth's surface. Once it reaches the surface, this magma is called lava. Lava can ooze out slowly or be flung violently into the sky alongside ash, rock, and deadly gases.

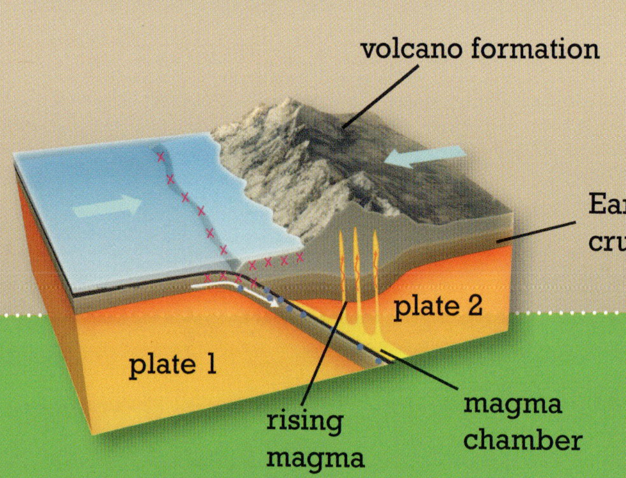

PLATE PRESSURE

Magma sits in large wells called magma chambers, which lie deep beneath the Earth's crust. The crust is formed of vast slabs of rock called tectonic plates, which are constantly moving.

When one plate moves over another, it pushes it down into the Earth's mantle. This causes some of the sinking plate's rock to melt into magma, which then rises to form a volcano. Volcanoes can also form in the gap where two plates move apart.

Magma from the magma chamber feeds into a volcano's main vent.

Magma lies in a chamber below the volcano, where it is under great pressure.

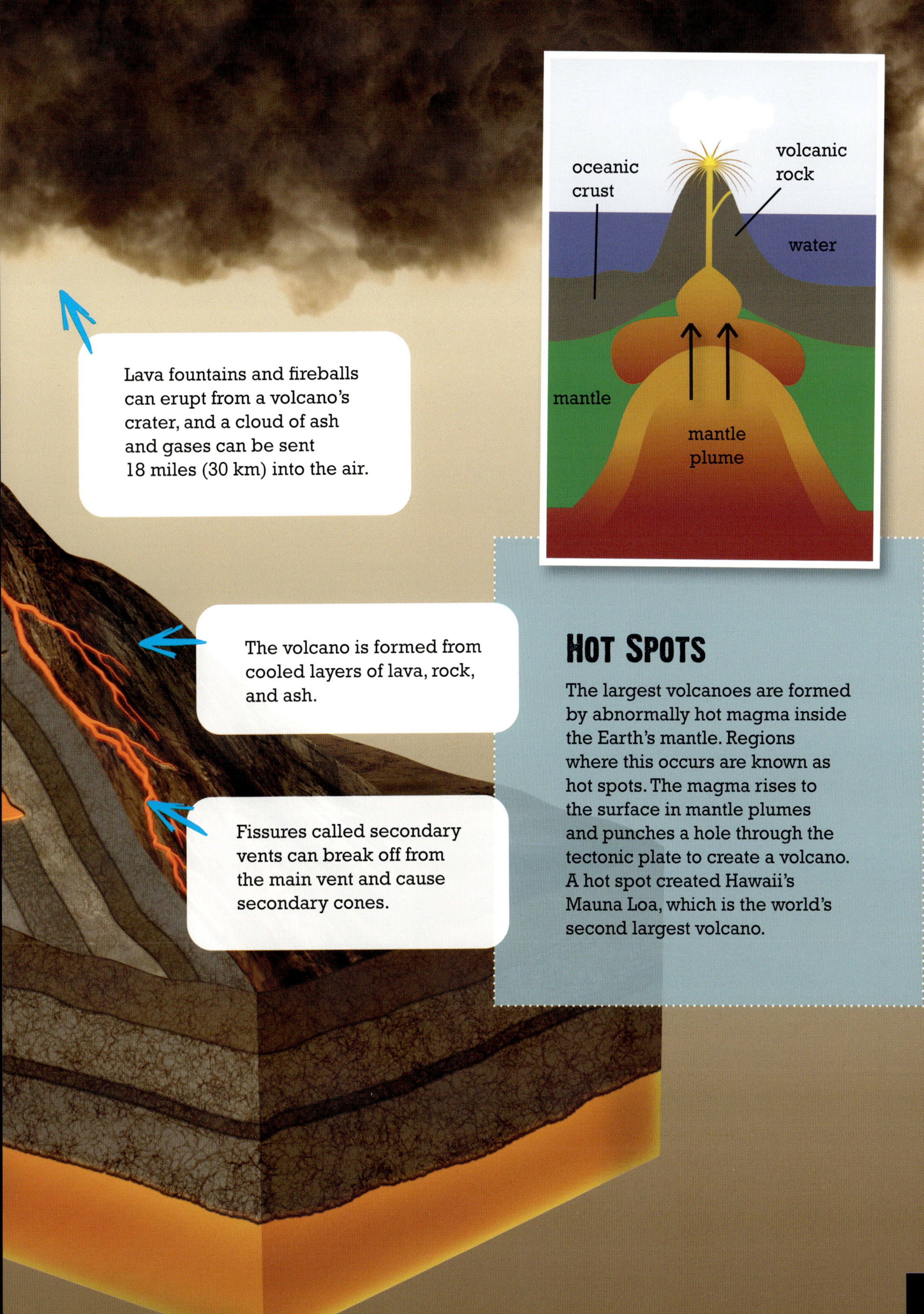

Hot Spots

The largest volcanoes are formed by abnormally hot magma inside the Earth's mantle. Regions where this occurs are known as hot spots. The magma rises to the surface in mantle plumes and punches a hole through the tectonic plate to create a volcano. A hot spot created Hawaii's Mauna Loa, which is the world's second largest volcano.

Types of Volcanoes

Volcanoes come in a variety of shapes and sizes, from simple cracks in the ground to majestic, cone-shaped mountains. A volcano's particular type is determined by the magma that feeds it. There are four main types of volcano: shield volcanoes, stratovolcanoes, cinder cones, and lava domes.

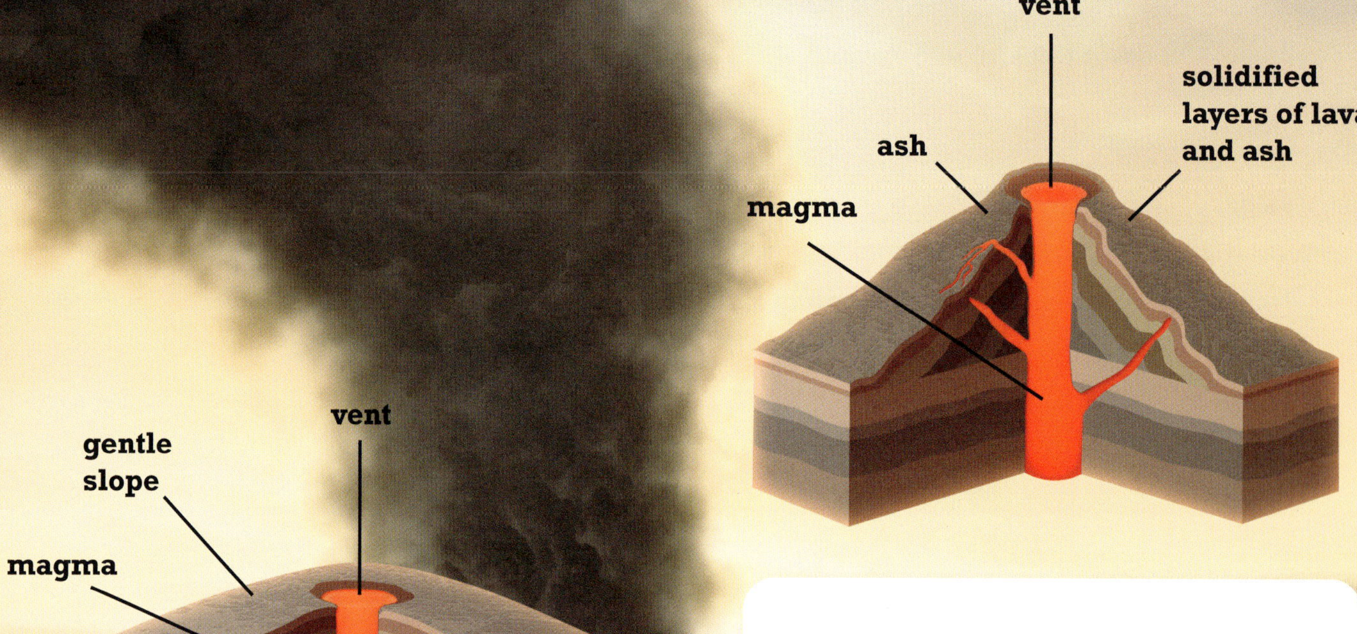

Stratovolcanoes

Built up from many layers of ash, rock, and sticky lava, stratovolcanoes, also called composite volcanoes, are formed by explosive eruptions. The eruptions occur when sticky lava prevents gas from escaping and causes pressure to build up. Over time, the erupted lava forms a cone shape.

Shield Volcano

Low and bowl-shaped, a shield volcano is formed from thin, runny lava, which flows down its gentle slopes and cools slowly. Because the lava is thin, it allows plenty of gas to escape with it. This prevents an explosive eruption.

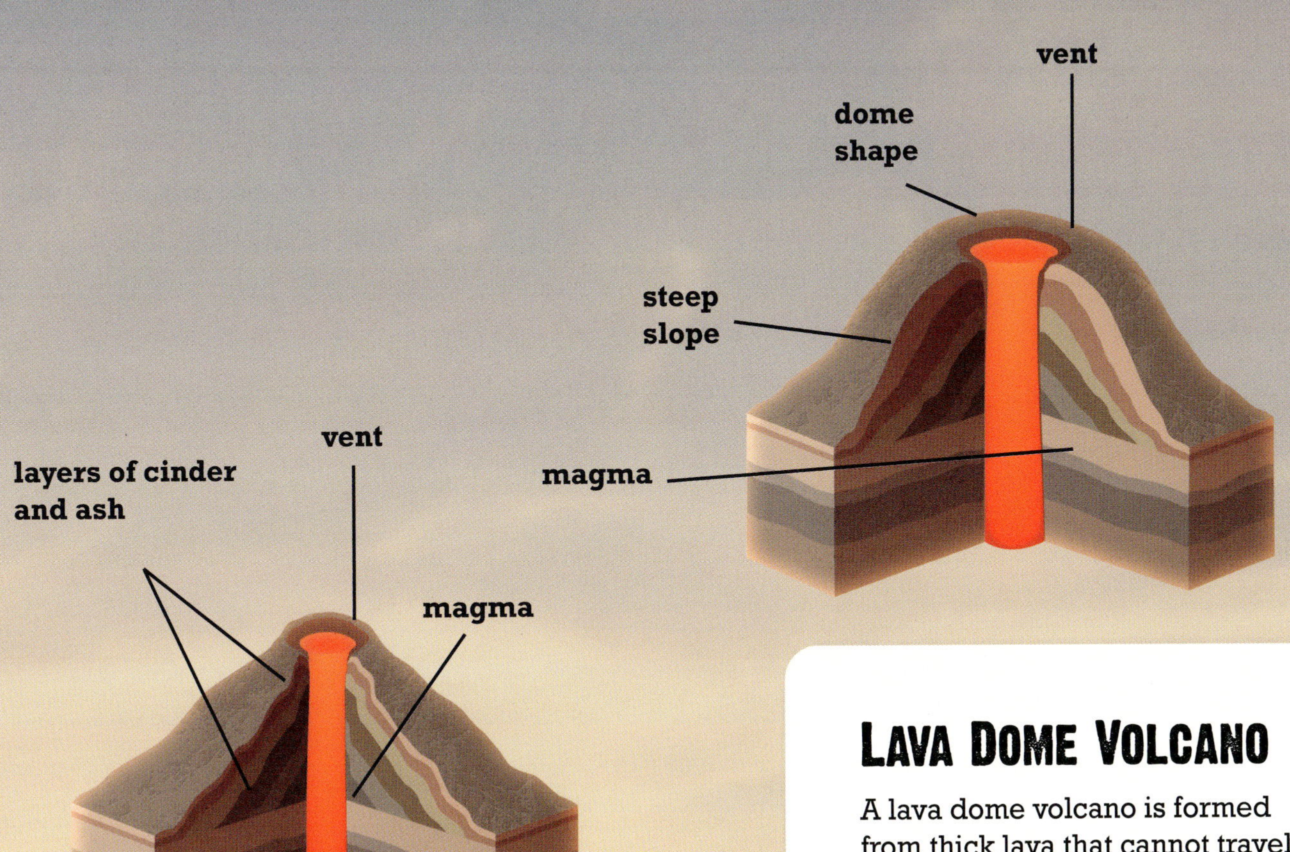

Lava Dome Volcano

A lava dome volcano is formed from thick lava that cannot travel far and simply piles up around its main vent. Hardened lava sometimes blocks the vent, leading to an explosion that blows off its top.

Cinder Cone Volcano

Cinder cone volcanoes are circular or oval-shaped and are formed from small pieces of lava and ash that blast into the air and cool after they reach the ground. The ash and lava then form layers around the top of the volcano's vent.

Active, Dormant, Extinct

Volcanoes are described as being active, dormant, or extinct. If a volcano is active, it erupts frequently. If it is classified as dormant, a volcano hasn't erupted in the past 10,000 years but is expected to erupt again. Extinct volcanoes are not expected to ever erupt again.

Rock, Gas, Ash, and Lava

The most explosive volcanic eruptions spew out rivers of lava, hurl "bombs" into the air, and release vast clouds of ash and toxic gases into the sky. Most deadly of all are the pyroclastic flows that rush down a volcano's slopes. Combined, these volcanic events can bring widespread destruction and a great loss of human life.

Lava Rivers

Lava can reach 2,282°F (1,250°C) in temperature. The two kinds of lava flows are called aa (pronounced *ah-ah*), which is filled with solid, angular lava chunks; and pahoehoe (pronounced *pah-hoey-hoey*), which is entirely liquid with a twisted, black skin on top.

Chunks of flying lava called bombs can range in size from a tennis ball to a house and can be thrown as far as 12 miles (20 km).

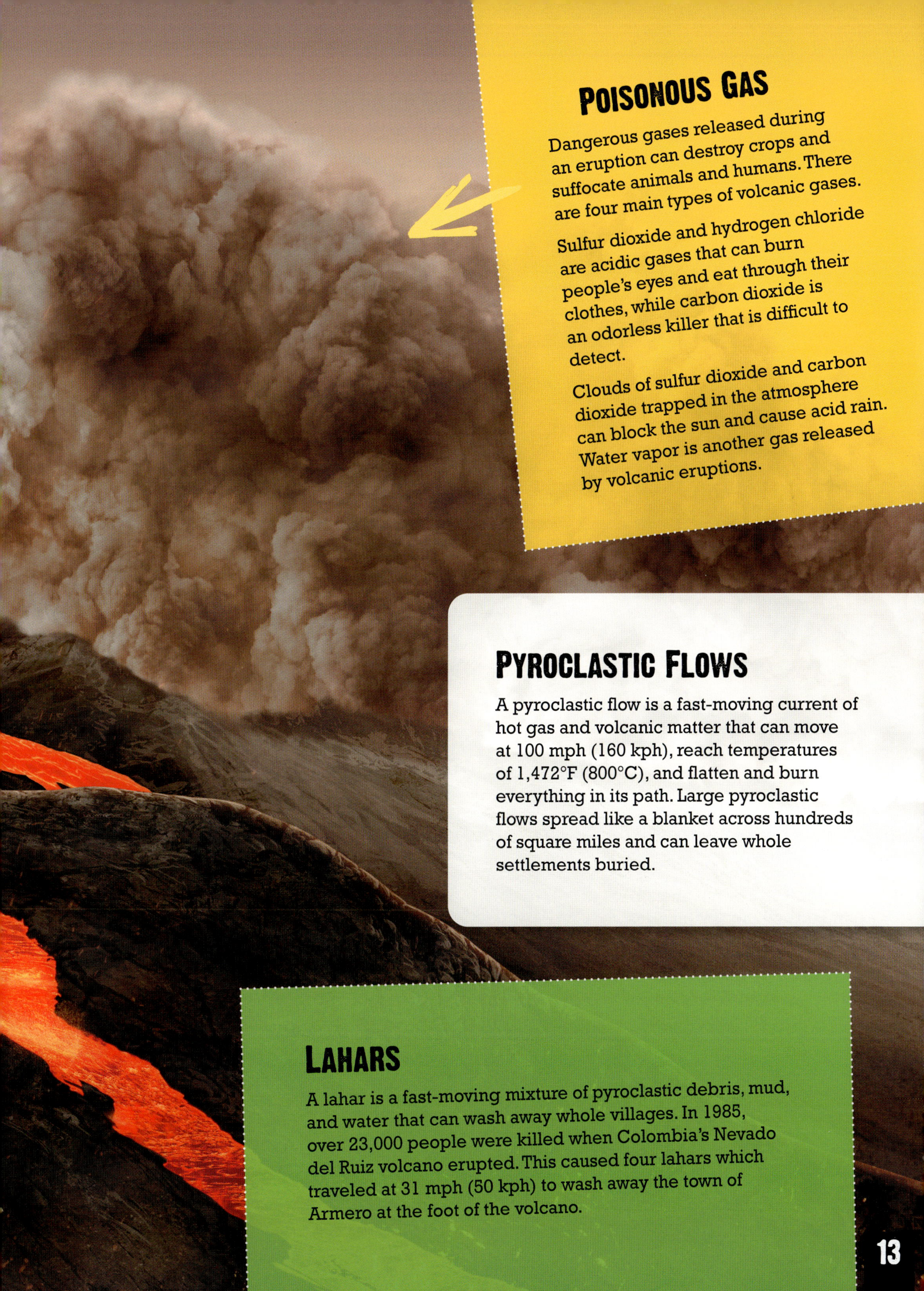

Poisonous Gas

Dangerous gases released during an eruption can destroy crops and suffocate animals and humans. There are four main types of volcanic gases.

Sulfur dioxide and hydrogen chloride are acidic gases that can burn people's eyes and eat through their clothes, while carbon dioxide is an odorless killer that is difficult to detect.

Clouds of sulfur dioxide and carbon dioxide trapped in the atmosphere can block the sun and cause acid rain. Water vapor is another gas released by volcanic eruptions.

Pyroclastic Flows

A pyroclastic flow is a fast-moving current of hot gas and volcanic matter that can move at 100 mph (160 kph), reach temperatures of 1,472°F (800°C), and flatten and burn everything in its path. Large pyroclastic flows spread like a blanket across hundreds of square miles and can leave whole settlements buried.

Lahars

A lahar is a fast-moving mixture of pyroclastic debris, mud, and water that can wash away whole villages. In 1985, over 23,000 people were killed when Colombia's Nevado del Ruiz volcano erupted. This caused four lahars which traveled at 31 mph (50 kph) to wash away the town of Armero at the foot of the volcano.

CASE STUDY: VESUVIUS, CE 79

History's most famous volcanic eruption took place in CE 79 near Naples in Italy. Here, Mount Vesuvius erupted over the Roman towns of Pompeii and Herculaneum, catching the local inhabitants completely unaware. Panic, deadly pyroclastic flows, and the extraordinary preservation of the towns followed.

ERUPTION

Vesuvius erupted at midday on August 24. Pumice, hot ash, and rock rained down on Pompeii and Herculaneum and turned the sky black as they blocked out the sun.

At midnight, a series of deadly pyroclastic flows surged down the volcano's slopes and engulfed the towns. The searing heat and suffocating gas killed over 2,000 people almost instantly. The towns were then buried under 23 feet (7 m) of volcanic debris.

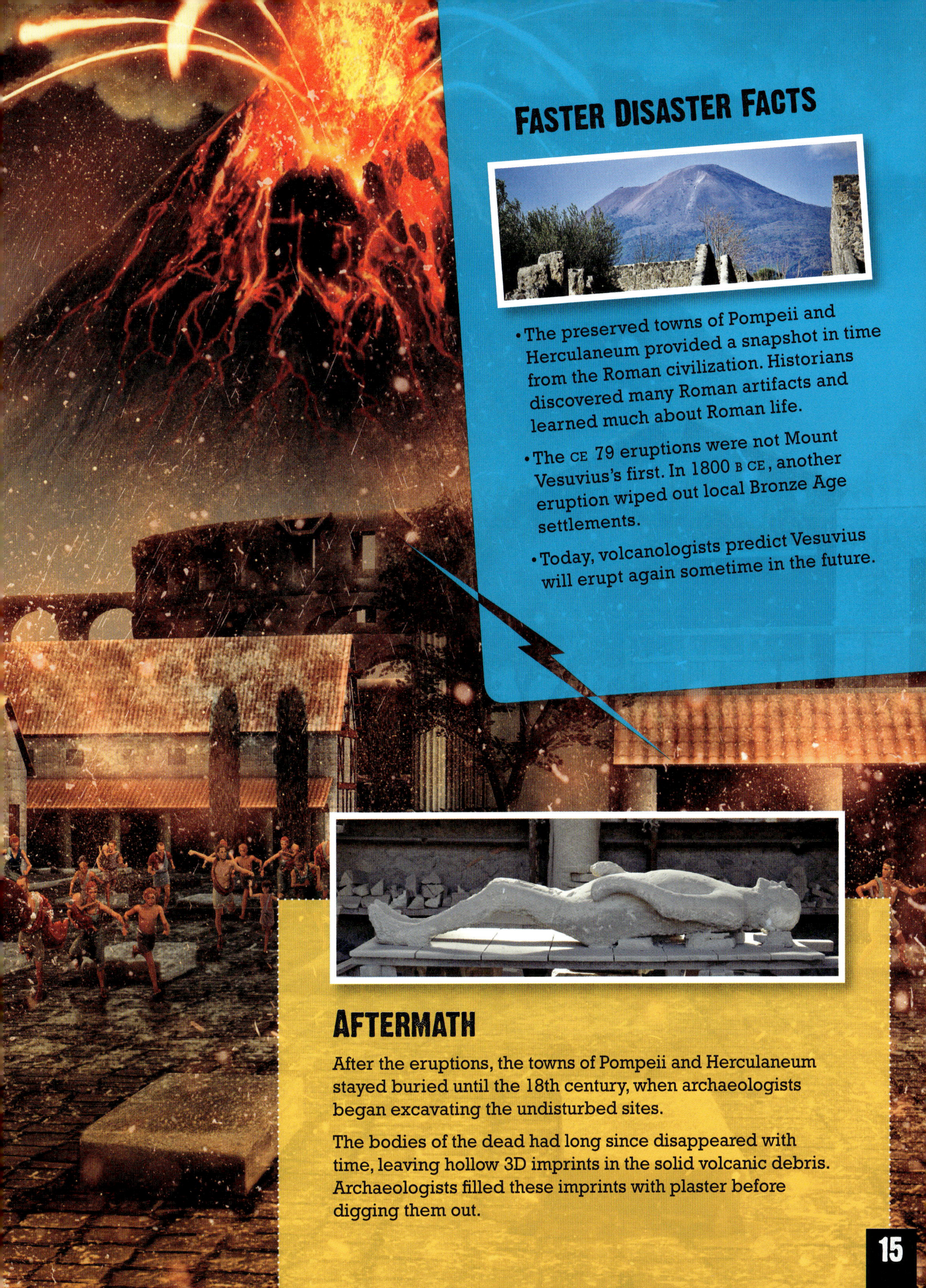

Faster Disaster Facts

- The preserved towns of Pompeii and Herculaneum provided a snapshot in time from the Roman civilization. Historians discovered many Roman artifacts and learned much about Roman life.
- The CE 79 eruptions were not Mount Vesuvius's first. In 1800 BCE, another eruption wiped out local Bronze Age settlements.
- Today, volcanologists predict Vesuvius will erupt again sometime in the future.

Aftermath

After the eruptions, the towns of Pompeii and Herculaneum stayed buried until the 18th century, when archaeologists began excavating the undisturbed sites.

The bodies of the dead had long since disappeared with time, leaving hollow 3D imprints in the solid volcanic debris. Archaeologists filled these imprints with plaster before digging them out.

SUPERVOLCANOES

Supervolcanoes are Earth's largest and most powerful volcanoes. An erupting supervolcano produces over 1,000 times more lava than a normal volcano. It can have a devastating impact on the Earth's ecology. However, no human has ever seen a supervolcano erupt. The last eruption took place 26,500 years ago.

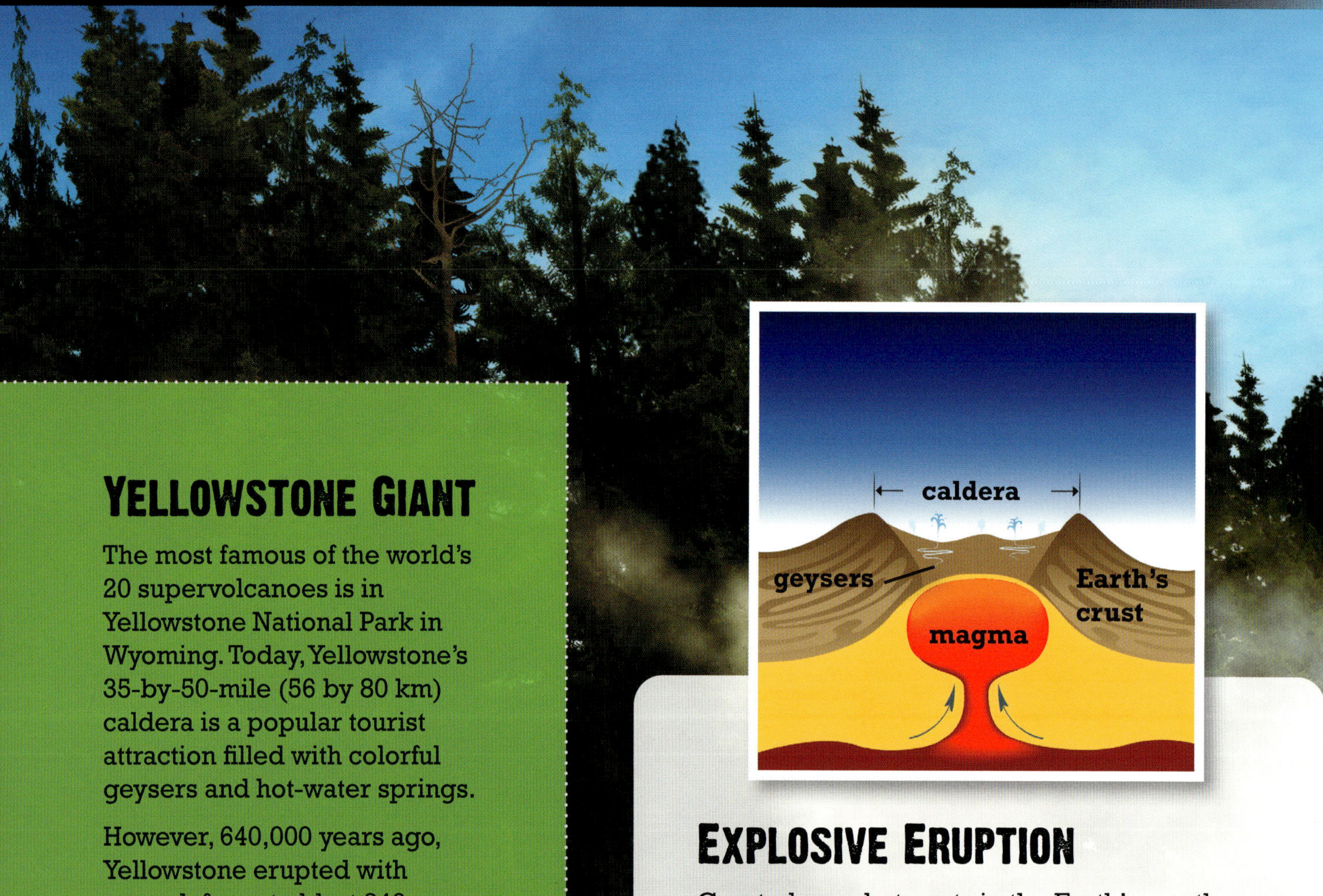

YELLOWSTONE GIANT

The most famous of the world's 20 supervolcanoes is in Yellowstone National Park in Wyoming. Today, Yellowstone's 35-by-50-mile (56 by 80 km) caldera is a popular tourist attraction filled with colorful geysers and hot-water springs.

However, 640,000 years ago, Yellowstone erupted with enough force to blast 240 cubic miles (1,000 cubic km) of lava, dust, and ash into the atmosphere. That is enough debris to bury a city to a depth of several miles.

EXPLOSIVE ERUPTION

Created over hot spots in the Earth's mantle, supervolcanoes usually erupt with such explosive power that the ground collapses and only a shallow crater called a caldera is left.

Deep below the caldera is a vast magma chamber with molten rock that is under intense pressure. When an eruption is imminent, this pressure becomes like trying to keep a ball underwater. In the end, the magma has no place to go but up.

PREDICT, NOT PREVENT

Scientists monitor Yellowstone carefully for signs of seismic activity. They hope there will be enough time to predict a future eruption because no one will be able to prevent it.

A Yellowstone eruption could cover the surrounding 500 miles (800 km) in 4 inches (10 cm) of ash and send an umbrella cloud of gases into the atmosphere that could block out the sun. This could cause severe climate change that would result in widespreadcrop failure and famine.

PEOPLE AND VOLCANOES

Expert scientists who travel around the world to study erupting volcanoes are called volcanologists. They do hot, dangerous work which involves getting closer to one of nature's most destructive forces than many would dare. By predicting when a volcano is about to erupt, volcanologists can help save the lives of those who live nearby.

TOOLS OF THE TRADE

Volcanologists rely on several tools to take samples from red-hot lava flows, monitor the poisonous gases escaping from the volcano's vent, measure tremors in the Earth, and stay safe.

NOTEBOOK

When a volcanologist arrives at a volcano, the first thing they do is make a full survey of the area. This involves drawing sketches and taking notes in a notebook. Laptops and digital cameras are also used. A special glass bottle on a pole is sometimes used to collect gas samples.

SAFETY SUIT

A proximity suit is a full-body, heat-shield suit that allows volcanologists to get close to a lava flow or the rim of an active volcano. The suit ensures no part of the body is exposed to lava flows, which can burn and blister skin. Heatproof boots also enable scientists to withstand extreme temperatures underfoot.

VOLCANO MONITORING

Volcano observatories have been built around the world to monitor local volcanoes. They provide updates based on new seismic activity and changes in gases expelled by volcanoes. Founded in 1814, the Vesuvius Observatory is the oldest volcano observatory in the world.

SEISMOMETER

Instruments that measure seismic activity, called seismometers, are one of a volcanologist's main tools for predicting eruptions. These are placed on or in the ground, where they send signals via a satellite internet connection. Tremors in the earth around a volcano often precede an eruption.

ROCK HAMMER

A volcanologist's most essential tool is a small rock hammer. This is used to chip off samples of rock and lava and collect them for analysis in a laboratory. Learning what rocks are made of and how they were formed is one of a volcanologist's main tasks.

When an Avalanche Is Released

On February 9, 2010, a freak storm struck the Hindu Kush mountainside above the Salang Pass, Afghanistan. Torrential rain and ferocious winds loosened the mountain snow and set off a series of avalanches that trapped drivers along the road and tunnel below. It became a race against time to dig the motorists out.

Bring in the Army

Afghan National Army helicopters were rushed to the avalanche site alongside 500 soldiers armed with shovels. They learned the storm had caused not one, but 17 avalanches above a 2-mile (3.5 km) stretch of road. It was reported that over 2,600 people were trapped in their vehicles beneath several feet of snow as well as inside the tunnel. Some vehicles had been swept off the road and down the mountain on the other side.

Rescue Mission

After digging out a bus, rescuers from a nearby village discovered 14 people still alive with 40 frozen bodies buried beneath them. Digging out those trapped in the Salang Tunnel proved difficult, and bulldozers were called in to help.

Although over 2,600 motorists were rescued, 175 lost their lives, making it one of Afghanistan's deadliest avalanches.

Faster Disaster Facts

- At 2 miles (3,400 m) above sea level, the Salang Pass is one of the highest roads in the world.
- The Salang Pass had previously been struck by a series of avalanches between 1993 and 2002.
- During the 2010 avalanches, some drivers inside the Salang Tunnel were believed to have died from carbon monoxide poisoning from their own car exhausts.

WHAT'S IN AN AVALANCHE?

An avalanche is a mass of unstable ice and snow that suddenly slides down a mountainside. Avalanches can reach speeds of 200 mph (320 kph) and contain enough force to sweep away people, knock over trees, and bury buildings. An avalanche can happen almost anywhere there is snow, a slope, and a trigger to set it off.

ANATOMY OF AN AVALANCHE

An avalanche is made up of three main parts. The **starting zone** is the section at the top of a mountain slope where the snow is most unstable. An avalanche begins when this snow breaks loose and begins to slide.

As the snow picks up speed, it collects more snow, ice, and rock and travels down a path known as the **track**. This is usually free of obstacles such as trees.

The snow finally comes to a stop and piles up in the bottom region, called the **runout zone**.

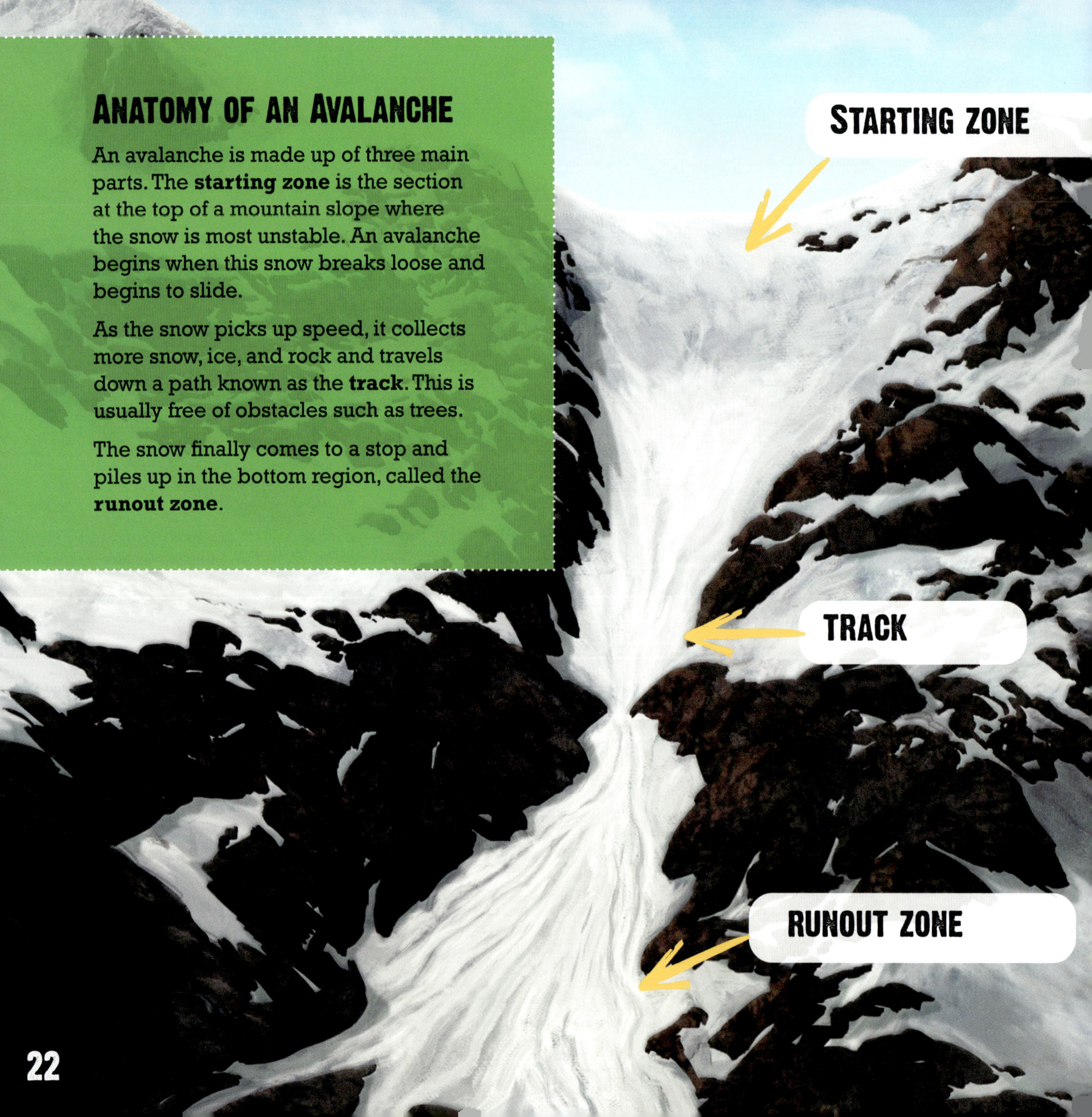

Snowpacks

Layers of snow are called snowpacks. Each layer contains a different kind of snow that has been formed by a particular type of weather.

Avalanche-prone snowpacks have layers of thin, weak snow, positioned between thicker layers of hard snow. This makes the whole snowpack unstable enough to cause an avalanche.

What Causes an Avalanche?

Avalanches are usually triggered by wind, rain, heavy snowfall, earthquakes, volcanoes, a rise in temperature, or human activity. The weight of someone skiing or walking can set off an avalanche, as can a snowmobile.

AVALANCHE TYPES

To the untrained eye, all avalanches look alike. However, there are two main types of avalanches: powder and slab. These types behave with different degrees of speed and power. Both are potentially deadly to humans unlucky enough to be caught by them.

POWDER AVALANCHE

Powdered snow is formed during very cold, dry weather. It is made up of snowflakes that do not bond together well, creating unstable snow. If this snow lies on a hard, icy layer of snow, then it becomes even more unstable.

Strong winds or new, heavy snowfalls can trigger avalanches of powdered snow. As the snow travels downward at speeds that can reach 200 mph (320 kph), it can accumulate to create snowballs.

SLAB AVALANCHE

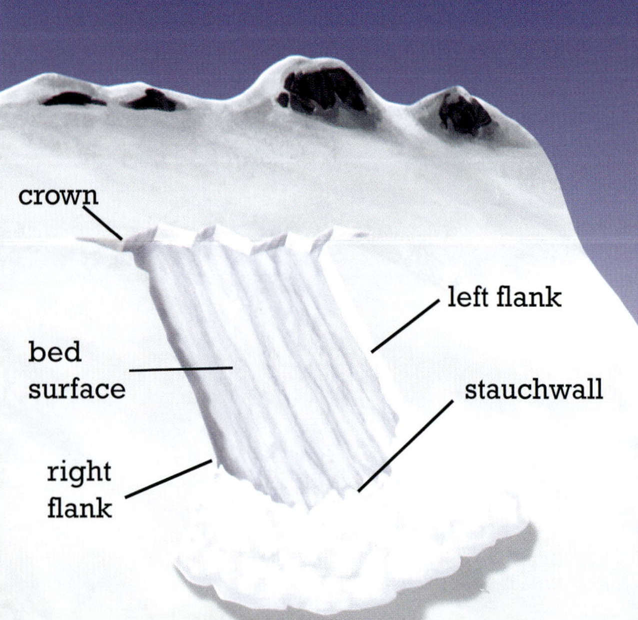

A slab avalanche starts off as a frozen layer of weak snow. When new, heavy snowfall lands on top of this layer, it forms another layer known as a slab. If a trigger, such as a skier or snowmobile, travels over this snow, they can break the weak layer below and cause the slab on top to slide downwards.

A slab avalanche can reach speeds of up to 80 mph (130 kph) within five seconds. As it descends downward, the slab often breaks up into smaller chunks, which are capable of destroying whole villages.

WET AVALANCHES

Wet avalanches occur when sunshine, warm air, or rain changes the chemical makeup of a snowpack and saturates it with water. This can create a slow-moving avalanche that seldom travels faster than 25 mph (40 kph). However, wet avalanches can be dense and heavy enough to cause great destruction.

People and Avalanches

Avalanches are unpredictable and difficult to monitor. Many happen in remote mountainous regions. However, in more built-up areas, scientists research avalanche-prone areas. This helps people avoid likely spots where an avalanche might happen.

Avalanche Warnings

Several countries have avalanche organizations that work to predict and prevent avalanches. To do this, scientists collect snow samples from mountainsides and study their different layers. The scientists then combine their findings with weather reports and release avalanche warnings in particular areas. The avalanche danger is given a rating between 1 (low) and 5 (extreme).

North American Public Avalanche Danger Scale

Avalanche danger is determined by the likelihood, size, and distribution of avalanches.

Danger Level		Travel Advice
Extreme		Avoid all areas where an avalanche could occur.
High		Very dangerous avalanche conditions. Do not travel in avalanche-prone areas.
Considerable		Dangerous avalanche conditions. Check snowpacks. Choose routes carefully and be cautious of avalanche-prone areas.
Moderate		Avalanche conditions are more likely in avalanche-prone areas. Check snowpacks. Identify routes and slopes where avalanches could occur.
Low		Generally safe avalanche conditions. Watch out for unstable snow on isolated slopes and in avalanche-prone areas.
No Rating		Watch out for and avoid slopes with recent avalanches or unstable snow. Signs include cracking in the snow and the sound of snowpacks collapsing.

Preventing Avalanches

Avalanches are often slowed or stopped in their tracks by large natural barriers such as forests. As a result, large tree-planting projects take place in avalanche risk areas.

People also build man-made barriers, such as fences made of wood and steel, above villages and towns to protect them. Fences built at angles on the slope hold back snow and stop it from forming large, single slabs.

Snow Studies

To study avalanches more closely, the simplest thing is to see inside one. To do this, the Swiss Federal Institute for Snow and Avalanche Research (SLF) has built underground observation bunkers on an avalanche-prone mountain slope in the Swiss Alps.

When a natural avalanche is not forthcoming, the SLF creates its own by dropping a 33-pound (15 kg) explosive from a helicopter. When the avalanche is released, scanning devices and cameras record data from inside the bunkers.

CASE STUDY: HUASCARAN, 1970

On May 31, 1970, the deadliest avalanche in modern history struck Peru. The avalanche was triggered by a powerful earthquake, which flattened dozens of Peruvian towns and villages. The quake also broke a vast section of glacial ice and rock free from a large volcano called Mount Huascaran. This caused the massive "Nevados Huascaran" avalanche to crash down the mountainside.

DEVASTATION

The avalanche traveled for 11 miles (18 km) as it thundered down Mount Huascaran. Ice mixed with rock and mud as the avalanche reached speeds of 208 mph (335 kph). The towns of Yungay and Ranrahirca, which sat at the bottom of Mount Huascaran, were completely buried beneath over 164 feet (50 m) of avalanche debris. Only 400 of Yungay's population of 18,500 survived. In Ranrahirca, 2,000 were killed.

RESCUE

It took over two days for rescue teams to reach the buried towns of Yungay and Ranrahirca. In the meantime, survivors had been searching for loved ones by digging out rubble with their bare hands. But instead of trying to dig out all of the dead bodies, the Peruvian government declared the site a mass grave. All future excavation at the site has been forbidden.

Fast Disaster Facts

- The Nevados Huascaran avalanche was made from a chunk of ice, snow, and rock 2,985 feet (910 m) wide and 1 mile (1.6 km) long.
- An estimated 2.8 billion cubic feet (80 million cubic m) of snow, rock, and mud landed on the towns of Yungay and Ranrahirca.
- The Great Peruvian Earthquake and the Nevados Huascaran claimed the lives of around 74,000 people and left 800,000 people homeless.
- May 31 is a remembrance day in Peru for the victims of this disaster.

Glossary, Books and Helpful Websites

Glossary

acid rain
Polluted rainfall that causes harm to the environment it falls on.

archipelago
A group of islands.

atmosphere
The layer of gases surrounding the Earth.

atomic bomb
A bomb that creates a violent explosion through the release of nuclear energy.

carbon monoxide
A colorless, odorless gas that is toxic to humans.

continents
Seven massive areas of land that make up the Earth's land.

debris
Pieces of garbage and the remains of buildings that are scattered everywhere.

displaced
Forced to leave home because of a disaster.

Earth's crust
The layer closest to the surface of our planet.

evacuation
The orderly removal of people from a place to avoid a disaster.

exclusion zone
An area where it is forbidden for people to go.

extinct
No longer alive, active, or in existence.

famine
A great lack of food over a wide area.

geyser
A hot spring that sends a column of hot water and steam into the air.

glacier
A slow-moving mass of ice formed on mountainsides.

incinerate
To destroy something by burning it.

magma
Molten rock flowing beneath the Earth's crust.

mantle
A layer of the Earth that makes up 85 percent of the entire planet. The mantle is mostly solid rock, but some parts are hotter and more fluid.

mantle plume
A column of hot rock that rises through the Earth's mantle.

observatory
A building dedicated to studying the stars or natural phenomena on Earth, such as volcanoes.

ocean basin
A large dip in the Earth's surface in which an ocean lies.

pumice
A very light volcanic rock made from bubbly lava.

satellite
An object that orbits a star or planet. Many Earth satellites are man-made objects that can take photos and record data about the planet.

tectonic plate
A moving section of Earth's crust.

BOOKS

Volcanoes (Write On) by Clare Hibbert (Franklin Watts, 2016)

The Science of Natural Disasters: The Devastating Truth about Volcanoes, Earthquakes and Tsunamis (Science of the Earth) by Alex Woolf (Franklin Watts, 2018)

Our Planet Earth (Cause, Effect and Chaos!) by Paul Mason (Wayland, 2018)

Landslides and Avalanches (Transforming Earth's Geography) by Joanna Brundle (KidHaven 2019)

HELPFUL WEBSITES

These websites for kids are all about volcanoes and avalanches:

www.natgeokids.com/uk/discover/geography/physical-geography/volcano-facts/

www.weatherwizkids.com/weather-volcano.htm

www.nationalgeographic.com/environment/natural-disasters/avalanches/

www.weatherwizkids.com/weather-safety-avalanche.htm

INDEX